BOSTON COMMON PRESS
Brookline, Massachusetts

1999

HOW TO
MAKE SOUP

An illustrated step-by-step guide to
preparing favorite stocks,
soups, and chowders.

THE COOK'S ILLUSTRATED LIBRARY

Illustrations by John Burgoyne

Boston Common Press
17 Station Street
Brookline, Massachusetts 02445

ISBN 0-936184-37-X
Library of Congress Cataloging-in-Publication Data
The Editors of *Cook's Illustrated*
      How to make soup: An illustrated step-by-step guide to preparing favorite stocks, soups, and chowders./The Editors of *Cook's Illustrated*
1st ed.

      Includes 30 recipes and 11 illustrations
      ISBN 0-936184-37-X (hardback): $14.95
      I. Cooking. I. Title
1999

Manufactured in the United States of America

Distributed by Boston Common Press, 17 Station Street, Brookline, MA 02445.

Cover and text design: Amy Klee
Recipe development: Kay Rentschler and Bridget Lancaster
Series editor: Jack Bishop

CONTENTS

introduction

THE ARGUMENT OVER WHETHER COOKING
is subjective or objective, a matter of indi-
vidual taste or scientific principle, comes
to a head in the preparation of soup. Few
cooks would claim independence from the laws of chem-
istry when baking a cake, but when throwing together a pot
of soup on a gray November day, one is tempted to throw
caution to the wind and simmer up whatever is in the vegetable bin that afternoon.

This reminds me of a gentleman in our town in
Vermont who was known for his lack of attention to natural
laws. On one occasion, while he was riding a tractor out of
gear down a steep driveway, the hay wagon he was pulling
ended up in twisted pieces across the road, but the tractor
remained upright, the driver no worse for the ride and as
unconcerned as ever about his brush with disaster.

I often feel like that headstrong neighbor of mine when
concocting a batch of soup. After all, what is there to know
about such a simple preparation? Well, having spent months

developing the recipes in this book, the staff of *Cook's Illustrated* can honestly say that there is a great deal to know if you want to turn out a great bowl of soup. Did you know that the best chicken stock is made by first sautéing chicken parts? that meat, not bones, is the key to success with beef stock? that many vegetables should be broiled to bring out the flavor in puréed soups? or that old Parmesan rinds are just the thing to enhance a minestrone? These prescriptions may seem simple—as indeed most of the techniques in this book are—but they can dramatically enhance flavor, the key to great soups.

How to Make Soup will provide you with the best recipes for chowder, split pea soup, lentil soup, potato-leek soup, and more. In learning the principles behind these recipes, you'll also learn to make your own soups from scratch.

How to Make Soup is the eighteenth book in a series of "how to" titles published by *Cook's Illustrated*, a bimonthly publication about American home cooking. Turn to the beginning of the book for a complete list of titles in our "how to" series. To order other books, call us at (800) 611-0759 or visit us on line at www.cooksillustrated.com. For a free trial copy of *Cook's*, call (800) 526-8442.

Christopher P. Kimball
Publisher and Editor
Cook's Illustrated

chapter one

SOUP BASICS

MAKING SOUP IS ONE OF THE EASIEST and most rewarding kitchen tasks. The basic ingredients—stock, onions, carrots, potatoes, and herbs—are almost always on hand. The technique is simple. Most recipes begin with the sautéing of aromatic vegetables to build flavor. Liquid is then added along with the distinguishing ingredients—tomatoes for cream of tomato soup or lentils for a lentil soup—and everything is simmered until tender.

Although this process sounds simple (and it is), there are a number of issues that require some special attention.

8

STOCK

Perhaps the most important issue that faces the cook when making soup is the choice of liquid. Without a doubt, homemade stock (usually chicken stock) is the best option. It has a rich flavor that complements not only chicken but also vegetables, grains, and beans. Certain recipes are best made with something other than chicken stock (as you will see in this book), but if you keep just one homemade stock on hand, make it chicken stock.

We find that beef stock has it uses, especially in a beef soup. It is also delicious (but not essential) in French onion soup. We understand the appeal of vegetable stock for vegetarians, but, given a choice, we always opt for chicken stock, even in a vegetable soup. Of course, if you don't eat meat, you can use vegetable stock, either homemade or store-bought, in any vegetable or bean soup recipe in this book and achieve fine results. In many cases, you could even use water. Soups made with water or vegetable stock will, however, taste less complex.

Our chicken stock takes just an hour to make and is worth the minimal effort. Unfortunately, even the most diligent cook may not always have the time to make homemade stock. Canned broths make good soups, especially if you follow some simple guidelines.

Avoid canned beef broths at all cost. We tested 11 leading brands of canned beef broth and beef bouillon cubes and could not find one that we liked. None really tasted like beef, and most had strong off flavors. Government regulations require makers of beef broth to use only 1 part protein to 135 parts moisture in their product. That translates into less than 1 ounce of meat to flavor 1 gallon of water. (In contrast, our homemade beef stock uses 6 pounds of meat and bones to flavor 2 quarts of water.) Most manufacturers use salt, monosodium glutamate (MSG), and yeast-based hydrolyzed soy protein to give their watery concoctions some flavor and mouthfeel. None of these cheap tricks works.

By comparison, canned chicken broth is far superior. In our tasting of 10 leading brands, we found several that actually tasted like chicken. However, many brands are overly salty, which may explain why low-sodium broths made by Campbell's and Swanson (both brands are owned by the same company) topped our ratings.

Most commercial brands of stock come in cans that measure just under two cups. (Aseptic paper containers generally hold a liter, or just more than four cups.) If using the smaller cans, just add a little water to stretch the broth as needed in recipes. For instance, if a recipe calls for four cups of broth, use two cans of broth plus a few extra ounces of water to make four cups.

STORING AND REHEATING SOUP

One of the beauties of soup is the fact that it holds so well. Make a pot on Sunday and you can enjoy soup several times during the week. Unless otherwise specified, all the soups in this book can be refrigerated for several days or frozen for several months. Store soup in an airtight container. When ready to serve, reheat only as much soup as you need at that time. You can reheat soup in the microwave or in a covered saucepan set over medium-low heat. Because the microwave heats unevenly, this method is best for single servings. Just heat the soup right in the serving bowl or mug. Larger quantities of soup are best reheated on the stovetop.

You may find that a soup has thickened in the refrigerator or freezer. (As soup cools, liquid evaporates in the form of steam.) Simply thin out the soup with a little water to achieve the proper texture.

While most soups can be cooled, then reheated without harm, some will suffer, especially in terms of texture. Soups with rice and pasta are best eaten immediately. When refrigerated, rice and pasta become mushy and bloated as they absorb the liquid in the soup. If you plan on having leftovers, cool the soup before adding the rice or pasta, which is often the last step in most recipes. Add a portion of the rice or pasta to the soup you plan on eating immediately, then add the rest when you reheat the remaining soup.

Soups with seafood also fail to hold up well. For instance, clams will become tough if overcooked by reheating. These soups are best served as soon as they are done.

Finally, pureed soups made from green vegetables will look their best if served immediately upon completion of the recipe. Reheating breaks down the chlorophyll in some green vegetables (asparagus is especially prone to this problem). A soup that is bright green can turn drab army green if stored for several hours and then reheated. Of course, these soups will still taste delicious, but their visual appeal will be greatly diminished.

EQUIPMENT

Soupmaking requires just a few pieces of equipment. At the most basic level, all you need is a pot and spoon. Here are our recommendations for all the equipment used in this book.

▝▞ SOUP KETTLE/DUTCH OVEN

Most soups can be prepared in a small stockpot (also called a soup kettle) or Dutch oven. These pots work best because they are generally quite large (at least seven quarts) and have two handles, which makes lifting much easier. Dutch ovens are twice as wide as they are high. For stockpots, the opposite is true—they are generally twice as high as they are wide.

Because of their different shapes, we find it slightly easier to sauté in a Dutch oven. There's more surface area, and the vegetables are easier to stir in a shallower pot. This greater surface area also causes soups simmered uncovered to reduce and condense more than they would in a stockpot.

Another consideration when choosing a pot for soup-making is cost. Most Dutch ovens are designed for making stews and braises and have thick, heavy bottoms that will ensure good results when browning meat. Consequently, most good Dutch ovens cost about $150. We found that cheaper Dutch ovens cause pan drippings to burn. For soup-making, though, you can get away with a cheaper stockpot because it is used mostly for simmering liquids. In most soup recipes, a cheap aluminum stock pot will deliver fine results. As an added advantage, these pots are lightweight and easy to carry from the stovetop to the counter or sink.

⠓ BLENDER

The texture of a pureed soup should be smooth and creamy. With this in mind, we tried pureeing these soups in a food mill, a food processor, and a regular countertop blender, as well as with a handheld immersion blender.

Forget using the food mill for this purpose. We tried all three blades (coarse, medium, and fine), and, in each case, the liquid ran right through the blade as we churned and churned only to produce baby food of varying textures. Once separated, the liquid and pureed solids could not be combined with a whisk.

The food processor does a decent job of pureeing, but some small bits of vegetables can be trapped under the blade and remain unchopped. Even more troubling is the tendency of a food processor to leak hot liquid. Fill the workbowl more than halfway and you are likely to see liquid running down the side of the food processor base. Even small quantities of soup must be pureed in batches, and that's a hassle.

The immersion blender has more appeal since this tool can be brought directly to the pot and there is no ladling of hot ingredients. However, we found that this kind of blender also leaves some chunks behind. If you don't mind a few lumps, use an immersion blender.

For perfectly smooth pureed soups, use a regular blender. As long as a little headroom is left at the top of the blender, there is never any leaking. Also, the blender blade does an excellent job with soups because it pulls ingredients down from the top of the container. No stray bits go untouched by the blade.

Depending on the amount of soup you have made, you may need to puree in two batches. A standard blender has a capacity of seven cups, but it is best not to puree more than five cups of soup at a time.

∷ STRAINER

Even after pureeing, many soups will still contain stray bits of vegetable solids. You can leave the soup as it is, but for a

14

more refined texture it is best to remove these tiny pieces.

We tested a variety of strainers to see which is best for this job. With its three layers of fine mesh, a chinois (a conical French strainer used in many restaurants) proved too fine. We found that the fine mesh holds back almost all of the solids and the resulting soup is too brothy. A regular mesh strainer holds back too little. In our opinion, it does no good to pass a pureed soup through a typical mesh strainer. We had the best results when we turned to a fine, round mesh strainer (see figure 1, below). It removed large bits of vegetables but allowed the pureed solids to pass through with the liquid.

⠿ LADLE

You will want a large ladle for serving soup. We find a ladle with a capacity of one cup to be the most useful.

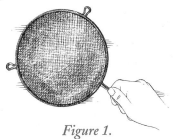

Figure 1.

The mesh on this strainer is fine enough to trap large solids but not so fine that it will hold back the pureed solids that should remain in a soup.

15

chapter two

CHICKEN SOUP

OST STANDARD CHICKEN STOCKS ARE not flavorful enough for a robust chicken soup. They are fine if ladled into risotto, but we wanted a broth that really tastes like chicken. We knew that the time-consuming conventional method—simmering chicken parts and aromatics such as onions, carrots, and celery in water for at least three hours—was part of the problem. This method takes so long to extract flavor from the chicken that many cooks shortcut the process and end up with weak stock. We wanted to see if we could do better in less time.

We tried blanching a whole chicken (cooking in boiling

16

water for several minutes) on the theory that blanching keeps the chicken from releasing foam during cooking and makes a clearer-tasting stock. The blanched chicken was then partially covered with water and placed in a heatproof bowl over a pan of simmering water. Cooked this way, the chicken itself was never simmered, and the resulting broth was remarkably clear, refined, and full-flavored. The only problem: it took four hours for the broth to take on sufficient flavor. We also noted that our four-pound chicken was good for nothing but the garbage bin after being cooked for so long.

A number of recipes favor roasting chicken bones or parts and then using them to make stock. The theory at work here is that roasted parts will flavor stock in minutes, not hours. We gave it a try several times, roasting chicken backs, necks, and bones, with and without vegetables. We preferred the roasted stock with vegetables but nonetheless found the actual chicken flavor to be too tame.

At last we tried a method described by Edna Lewis in her book *In Pursuit of Flavor* (Knopf, 1988). She sautés a chicken that's been hacked into small pieces along with an onion until the chicken loses its raw color. The pot is then covered, and the chicken and onion cook, or "sweat," over low heat until they release their rich, flavorful juices, which takes about 20 minutes. Only at that point is the water added, and the broth is simmered for just 20 minutes longer.

We knew we were onto something as we smelled the chicken and onions sautéing. The finished broth confirmed what our noses had detected, tasting pleasantly sautéed, not boiled. But we still had some refining to do: for once, we had made too strong a broth.

We substituted chicken backs and wing tips for the whole chicken and used more water. The resulting broth was less intense, just the right strength to make a base for some of the best chicken soup we've ever tasted. We made the stock twice more—once without the onion and once with onion, celery, and carrot. The onion added a flavor dimension we liked; the extra vegetables neither added nor detracted from the final soup, so we left them out.

After much trial and error, we had a master recipe that delivered liquid gold in just 40 minutes. While this recipe requires more hands-on work (hacking up parts, browning an onion, then chicken parts), it is ready in a fraction of the time required to make stock by traditional methods.

Where can you find these otherwise mostly useless chicken parts? The Buffalo chicken wing fad has made wings more expensive than legs and thighs. For those who can find chicken backs, this is clearly an inexpensive way to make stock for soup. Our local grocery store usually sells them for almost nothing, but in many locations they may be hard to get.

Luckily, we found that relatively inexpensive whole legs make incredibly full-flavored broths for soup. In a side-by-side comparison of two stocks, one made from backs and the other from whole legs, we found the whole leg broth to be even more full-flavored than the all-bone stock. Just don't try to salvage the meat from the legs. After 5 minutes of sautéing, 20 minutes of sweating, and another 20 minutes of simmering, the meat is void of flavor.

If you are making a soup that needs some chicken meat, use a whole chicken, as directed in the recipe for Chicken Stock with Sautéed Breast Meat (see page 24). The breast is removed, split into two pieces, sautéed briefly, and then added with the water to finish cooking. The rest of the bird—the legs, back, wings, and giblets—is sweated with the onions and discarded when the stock is done. The breast meat comes out of the pot perfectly cooked, ready to be skinned and shredded when cool. We particularly liked the tidiness of this method: one chicken yields one pot of soup.

One note about this method. We found it necessary to cut the chicken into pieces small enough to release their flavorful juices in a short period of time. A meat cleaver, a heavy-duty chef's knife, or a pair of heavy-duty kitchen shears makes the task fairly simple. Precision is not required. The point is to get the pieces small enough to release their flavorful juices in a short period of time.

To cut up a whole chicken, start by removing the whole legs and wings from the body; set them aside. Separate the back from the breast, then split the breast and set the halves aside. Hack the back crosswise into three or four pieces, then halve each of these pieces. Cut the wing at each joint to yield three pieces. Leave the wing tip whole, then halve each of the remaining joints. Because of their larger bones, the legs and thighs are the most difficult to cut. Start by splitting the leg and thigh at the joint, then hack each to yield three to four pieces.

Chicken Stock
makes about 2 quarts

➤ NOTE: *A cleaver will quickly cut up the chicken parts. A chef's knife will also work, albeit more slowly.*

1	tablespoon vegetable oil
1	medium onion, cut into medium dice
4	pounds chicken backs and wing tips or whole legs, hacked with cleaver into 2-inch pieces
2	quarts boiling water
2	teaspoons salt
2	bay leaves

■ INSTRUCTIONS:

1. Heat oil in large stockpot over medium heat. Add onion; sauté until colored and softened slightly, 2 to 3 minutes. Transfer onion to large bowl.

2. Add half of chicken pieces to pot; sauté until no longer pink, 4 to 5 minutes. Transfer cooked chicken to bowl with onion. Sauté remaining chicken pieces. Return onion and chicken pieces to pot. Reduce heat to low, cover, and cook until chicken releases its juices, about 20 minutes.

3. Increase heat to high; add boiling water, salt, and bay leaves. Return to simmer, then cover and barely simmer until broth is rich and flavorful, about 20 minutes.

4. Strain broth and discard solids. Skim fat (see figure 2, below, and figure 3, right) and reserve for later use in soups or other recipes, if desired. (Broth can be covered and refrigerated up to 2 days or frozen for several months.)

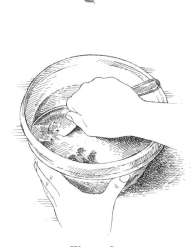

Figure 2.
Stock should be defatted before being used. The easiest way to do this is to refrigerate the stock until the fat rises to the surface and congeals. Use a spoon to scrape the fat off the surface. If you like, reserve the fat in an airtight container and use it in place of oil when sautéing.

Figure 3.

You won't always have time to refrigerate stock and wait for the fat to solidify. If this is the case, use a gravy skimmer (above right). Pour some stock into the skimmer, then pour the stock out through the spout attached to the bottom of the skimmer into a clean container. The fat will float to the top of the gravy skimmer as you pour. When there's nothing but a little fat left in the skimmer, remove the fat and start again with more stock. Repeat this process until the entire batch of stock has been defatted.

Chicken Stock with Sautéed Breast Meat
makes about 2 quarts

➤ NOTE: *Choose this broth when you want to add breast meat to soup. This recipe starts with a whole chicken rather than just backs or legs.*

1	tablespoon vegetable oil
1	whole chicken (about 3½ pounds), breast removed, split, and reserved; remaining chicken hacked with cleaver into 2-inch pieces
1	medium onion, cut into medium dice
2	quarts boiling water
2	teaspoons salt
2	bay leaves

▐ INSTRUCTIONS:

1. Heat oil in large stockpot over medium heat. When oil shimmers and starts to smoke, add chicken breast halves; sauté until brown on both sides, about 5 minutes. Remove chicken breast pieces and set aside. Add onion to pot; sauté until colored and softened slightly, 2 to 3 minutes. Transfer onion to large bowl.

2. Add half of hacked chicken pieces to pot; sauté until no

24

longer pink, 4 to 5 minutes. Transfer cooked chicken to bowl with onion. Sauté remaining hacked chicken pieces. Return onion and chicken pieces (excluding the breasts) to pot. Reduce heat to low, cover, and cook until chicken releases its juices, about 20 minutes.

3. Increase heat to high; add boiling water, chicken breasts, salt, and bay leaves. Return to simmer, then cover and barely simmer until chicken breasts are cooked through and broth is rich and flavorful, about 20 minutes.

4. Remove chicken breasts from pot; when cool enough to handle, remove skin from breasts, then remove meat from bones and shred into bite-sized pieces; discard skin and bone. Strain broth into separate container and discard solids. Skim fat (see figures 2 and 3, pages 22 and 23), and reserve for later use in soups or other recipes. (The shredded chicken and broth can be covered and refrigerated separately up to 2 days.)

Egg Drop Soup
serves six to eight

➤ **NOTE:** *Real egg drop soup starts with the finest home-made chicken stock. With stock made, the soup can be ready in just five minutes.*

1   recipe Chicken Stock (page 21)
1   tablespoon soy sauce
     Salt
2   tablespoons cornstarch
4   medium scallions, sliced thin
2   tablespoons minced fresh cilantro leaves
4   large eggs, beaten in a small bowl

INSTRUCTIONS:

1. Bring stock to simmer in large saucepan over medium-high heat. Add soy sauce and salt to taste.

2. Combine cornstarch and 2 tablespoons water in small bowl and stir until smooth. Whisk cornstarch mixture into broth until it thickens slightly. Stir in scallions and cilantro.

3. Whisk broth so that it is moving in circular direction in pan. Pour eggs into broth in slow, steady stream so that ribbons of coagulated egg form (see figure 4, right). Remove whisk and let eggs stand in broth without mixing until set, about 1 minute. Once set, break eggs up with a fork and serve soup immediately.

VARIATION:

Stracciatella

This Italian version of egg drop soup has grated Parmesan added to the broth.

Follow recipe for Egg Drop Soup, omitting soy sauce in step 1. Omit step 2 (that is, do not use cornstarch, scallions, or cilantro). Instead, beat ¼ cup grated Parmesan cheese and ¼ cup minced fresh basil leaves with eggs in measuring cup. Stir egg mixture into broth as directed in step 3. Season soup with ground black pepper before serving.

Figure 4.
Whisk the chicken broth so that it moves in a circular motion in the saucepan. Pour the beaten eggs into the broth in a slow, steady stream, whisking all the time, so that ribbons of coagulated egg form.

Chicken Noodle Soup
serves six to eight

➤ **NOTE:** *This recipe relies on stock made with breasts to provide some meat for the soup. To reinforce the poultry flavor, sauté the vegetables in chicken fat skimmed from cooled stock. Vegetable oil may used if you prefer.*

2	tablespoons chicken fat or vegetable oil
1	medium onion, cut into medium dice
1	large carrot, peeled and sliced ¼-inch thick
1	celery stalk, sliced ¼-inch thick
½	teaspoon dried thyme leaves
1	recipe Chicken Stock with Sautéed Breast Meat (page 24)
2	cups (3 ounces) wide egg noodles
¼	cup minced fresh parsley leaves
	Ground black pepper

⸬ **INSTRUCTIONS:**

1. Heat chicken fat in stockpot or Dutch oven over medium-high heat. Add onion, carrot, and celery; sauté until softened, about 5 minutes. Add thyme along with stock and shredded chicken meat; simmer until vegetables are tender and flavors meld, 10 to 15 minutes.

2. Add noodles and cook until just tender, about 5 minutes.

28

Stir in parsley and pepper to taste, adjust seasonings, and serve immediately.

::VARIATIONS:

Chicken Soup with Orzo and Spring Vegetables
Follow recipe for Chicken Noodle Soup, replacing onion with 1 medium leek, rinsed thoroughly, quartered lengthwise, then sliced thin crosswise. Substitute ½ cup orzo for egg noodles. Along with orzo, add ¼ pound trimmed asparagus, cut into 1-inch lengths, and ¼ cup fresh or frozen peas. Substitute 2 tablespoons minced fresh tarragon leaves for parsley.

Chicken Soup with Shells, Tomatoes, and Zucchini
Follow recipe for Chicken Noodle Soup, adding 1 medium zucchini, cut into medium dice, along with onion, carrot, and celery, and increase sautéing time to 7 minutes. Add ½ cup chopped tomatoes (fresh or canned) along with stock. Substitute 1 cup small shells or macaroni for egg noodles and simmer until noodles are cooked, about 10 minutes. Substitute an equal portion of fresh basil for parsley. Serve with grated Parmesan, if you like.

chapter three

BEEF SOUP

EEF STOCK SHOULD TASTE LIKE BEEF—ALMOST as intense as pot roast jus or beef stew broth—and be flavorful enough to need only a few vegetables and a handful of noodles or barley to make a good soup.

We began our testing by making a traditional stock using four pounds of beef bones fortified with a generous two pounds of beef, as well as celery, carrot, onion, tomato, and fresh thyme, all covered with four quarts of water. Our plan was to taste the stock after 4, 6, 8, 12, and 16 hours of simmering.

At hours 4, 6, and even 8, our stock was weak and tasted mostly of vegetables. And while the texture of the 12- and

16-hour stocks was richly gelatinous, the flavors of vegetables and bones (not beef) predominated.

Knowing now that it was going to take more meat than bones to get great flavor, we started our next set of tests by making broths with different cuts of meat, including chuck, shank, round, arm blade, oxtail, and short ribs. We browned two pounds of meat and one pound of small marrowbones, and we browned three pounds each of different bone-in cuts, such as shank, short ribs, and oxtails. We browned an onion along with each batch. After browning we covered the ingredients and let them "sweat" for 20 minutes. We added only a quart of water to each pot and simmered until the meat in each pot was done.

After a simmer of 1½ hours, our broths were done, most tasting unmistakably beefy. Upon a blind tasting of each, we agreed that the shank broth was our favorite, followed by the marrowbone-enhanced brisket and chuck. Not only was the broth rich, beefy, and full of body, the shank meat was soft and gelatinous, perfect for shredding and adding to a pot of soup (see figure 5, page 35). Because it appeared that our broth was going to require a generous amount of meat, the brisket's high price ($3.99 per pound compared with $1.99 for both the shanks and the chuck) knocked it out of the running.

Though not yet perfect, this broth was on its way to fulfilling our requirements. It could be made from common supermarket cuts like shank, chuck, and marrowbones. Second, it didn't take all day. This broth was done in about 2½ hours and was full-flavored as soon as the meat was tender. Unlike traditional stocks, which require a roasting pan, stockpot, oven, and burner, this was a one-pot, stovetop-only affair. Finally, this broth didn't require a cornucopia of vegetables to make it taste good. To us, the more vegetables, the weaker the beef flavor. At this point, our recipe called for one lone onion.

What we sacrificed in vegetables, however, we were going to have to compensate for in meat. It took two pounds of meat and one pound of bones to make a quart of broth.

At this point our richly flavored broth needed enlivening. Some broth recipes accomplish this with a splash of vinegar, others with tomato. Although we liked tomatoes in many of the soups we developed, they didn't do much for our broth. And although vinegar was an improvement, red wine made the broth taste even better. We ultimately fortified our broth with a modest half-cup of red wine, adding it to the kettle after browning the meat.

What we had done in developing our recipe for beef broth was to follow our method for making chicken broth—browning and then sweating a generous portion of meat and bones, adding water just to cover, and simmering for a relatively short time—without giving it much thought.

We knew the ratio of meat to water was right, but we wondered if it was really necessary to sweat the meat for 20 minutes before adding water. Side-by-side tests proved that sweating the meat did result in a richer-flavored broth. Moreover, the sweated meat and bones did not release foamy scum, thus eliminating the need to skim.

After much testing, we came to this inescapable conclusion: if you want to make beef soup right, you can't skimp on the meat.

Rich Beef Stock
makes scant 2 quarts

➤ **N O T E :** *Because meat makes such an important contribution to the flavor of this broth, a generous amount is required. For the recipes that follow, you will need only half the amount of meat used to make the broth. Refrigerate the leftover meat in an airtight container and use it for sandwiches or cold salads. If you prefer, replace the shank with 4 pounds of chuck cut into 1½-inch chunks and 2 pounds of small marrowbones.*

2	tablespoons vegetable oil
6	pounds shank, meat cut from bone in large chunks (see figure 5, page 35)
1	large onion, halved
½	cup dry red wine
½	teaspoon salt

I N S T R U C T I O N S :

1. Heat 1 tablespoon oil in large stockpot or Dutch oven over medium-high heat. Brown meat, bones, and onion halves on all sides in batches, making sure not to overcrowd pot and adding more oil to pot as necessary. Remove meat, bones, and onion and set aside. Add red wine to empty pot and cook until reduced to a syrup, 1 to 2 minutes. Return browned bones, meat, and onion to pot. Reduce heat to low, then cover and sweat meat and onion until they have released about ¾ cup dark, very intensely flavored liquid, about 20 minutes. Increase heat to medium-high, add 2 quarts water and salt, and bring to a simmer. Reduce heat to very low, partially cover, and barely simmer until meat is tender, 1½ to 2 hours.

2. Strain broth, discard bones and onion, and set meat aside. Skim fat from stock (see figures 2 and 3, pages 22 and 23) and discard. (Stock and meat to be used in soup can be refrigerated up to 5 days.)

Figure 5.
Cut the meat away from the shank bone in the largest possible pieces.

Beef Noodle Soup

serves six

➤ **NOTE:** *Our beef stock is the basis of a quick noodle soup.*

1	tablespoon vegetable oil
1	medium onion, cut into medium dice
2	medium carrots, cut into medium dice
1	celery stalk, cut into medium dice
½	teaspoon dried thyme or 1½ teaspoons minced fresh thyme leaves
½	cup canned diced tomatoes
1	recipe Rich Beef Stock, with 2 cups meat shredded into bite-sized pieces
2	cups (3 ounces) wide egg noodles
¼	cup minced fresh parsley leaves
	Salt and ground black pepper

INSTRUCTIONS:

1. Heat oil in stockpot or Dutch oven over medium-high heat. Add onion, carrots, and celery; sauté until softened, about 5 minutes. Add thyme and tomatoes, then beef broth and meat; bring to a simmer. Reduce heat to low and simmer until vegetables are no longer crunchy, about 15 minutes.

2. Add noodles and simmer until fully cooked, about 5 minutes longer. Stir in parsley, add salt and pepper to taste, and serve immediately.

Beef Barley Soup with Mushrooms
serves six

➤ NOTE: *Use any wild or domestic mushroom in this soup.*

2 tablespoons vegetable oil

1 medium onion, cut into medium dice

2 medium carrots, cut into medium dice

12 ounces mushrooms, sliced thin

½ teaspoon dried thyme or 1½ teaspoons minced fresh thyme leaves

½ cup canned diced tomatoes

1 recipe Rich Beef Stock, with 2 cups meat shredded into bite-sized pieces

½ cup pearl barley

¼ cup minced fresh parsley leaves
Salt and ground black pepper

▪▪ INSTRUCTIONS:

1. Heat oil in stockpot or Dutch oven over medium-high heat. Add onion and carrots; sauté until almost soft, 3 to 4 minutes. Add mushrooms and sauté until softened and liquid is almost completely evaporated, 4 to 5 minutes longer.

2. Add thyme and tomatoes, then beef broth, meat, and barley; bring to a simmer. Reduce heat to low and simmer until barley is just tender, 45 to 50 minutes. Stir in parsley, add salt and pepper to taste, and serve immediately.

chapter four

FRENCH ONION SOUP

RENCH ONION SOUP SHOULD HAVE A DARK,
rich broth, intensely flavored by a plethora of
seriously cooked onions, covered by an oversized crouton that is broth-soaked beneath
and cheesy and crusty on top. The first obstacle to success
is the broth. This soup is most commonly made with homemade beef stock (see page 34). But making beef stock takes
at least three hours. We wondered if there was a way to get
around this step.

We tested soups made with chicken stock, both homemade (which takes considerably less time to prepare than
beef stock) and canned. Both were, well, too chicken-y and

just not right. Soups made with canned beef broth were terrible. Canned beef broth does not have enough flavor to carry the day alone. After experimentation, we devised a formula for what we call cheater broth. By combining canned beef and chicken broths with red wine (the secret ingredient here), we came up with a broth that has enough good, rich flavor to make an excellent soup base.

The next obvious step was to examine the onion factor. After a crying game of slicing many onions of several varieties and then sautéing away, we found Vidalias to be disappointingly bland and boring, white onions to be candy sweet and one-dimensional, and yellows to be only mildly flavorful, with just a slight sweetness. Red onions ranked supreme. Their flavor was intensely onion-y, sweet yet not cloying, and subtly complex.

What was exasperating about the onions is that they took nearly an hour to caramelize. On top of that, they required frequent stirring to keep them from sticking to the bottom of the pot and burning. We found that adding salt to the onions as they began to cook helped draw out some of the water and shaved about 10 minutes off the cooking time. But we began to wonder if it was necessary for the onions to be so caramelized.

We tried, as one recipe suggested, sautéing them until just softened and colored, but they didn't brown enough to contribute much flavor to the soup. Maybe, we thought, a vigorous sauté, over high heat to achieve deep browning, would do the trick. Not so. Onions cooked that way did not lose enough liquid and made the soup watery and bland. (Besides, there is something wrong with an onion soup in which the onions have even a hint of crunch.) We also tried roasting the onions, thinking that the even, constant heat of the oven might be the answer. Wrong again. Taking the pan in and out of the oven to stir the onions was an incredible hassle.

It was inattentiveness that caused us to let the drippings in the pot of a batch of onions go a little too far. The onions themselves, though soft, were not thoroughly caramelized, but all the goo stuck on the pot was. We were sure that the finished soup would taste burned, but we were surprised to find that it was, in fact, as sweet, rich, and flavorful as the soups we had been making with fully caramelized onions. To refine the technique we had stumbled on, we decided that medium-high heat was the way to go and that the drippings should be very, very deeply browned. There's no way around frequent stirring, but this method cut about another 10 minutes off the onion-cooking time, bringing it down to just over 30 minutes.

With all those wonderful, tasty drippings stuck to the bottom of the pot, the deglazing process—adding liquid and scraping up all the browned bits—is crucial. Once the broth is added to the onions, we found that a simmering time of 20 minutes is needed to allow the onion flavor to permeate the broth and the flavors to meld.

Some recipes call for placing the crouton in the bottom of the bowl and ladling the soup over it. We disagree. We opt to set the crouton on top, so that only its bottom side is moistened with broth while its top side is crusted with cheese. The crouton can then physically support the cheese and prevent it from sinking into the soup. To keep as much cheese as possible on the surface, we found it best to use two croutons, instead of only one, to completely fill the mouth of the bowl. A baguette can be cut on the bias as necessary to secure the closest fit.

Traditionally, French onion soup is topped with Swiss, Gruyère, or Emmentaler. Plain Swiss cheese was neither outstanding nor offensive. It was gooey, bubbly, and mild. Both Gruyère and Emmentaler melted to perfection and were sweet, nutty, and faintly tangy, but they were also very strong and pungent, overwhelming many tasters' palettes.

We found that the flavor of Swiss cheese could be improved with the addition of some grated Asiago cheese. Like Gruyère and Emmentaler, Asiago has a sweet and nutty flavor, but without the pungent quality. Parmesan was a good complement for the Swiss cheese, too, with a pleasant sweetness and saltiness, but without the nuttiness of Asiago.

French Onion Soup

serves 6

➤ NOTE: *For a soup that is resplendent with deep, rich flavors, use 8 cups of Rich Beef Stock (page 34) in place of the canned chicken and beef broths and red wine. Tie the parsley and thyme sprigs together with kitchen twine so they will be easy to retrieve from the soup pot.*

2	tablespoons unsalted butter
5	medium red onions (about 3 pounds), sliced thin
	Salt
6	cups low-sodium canned chicken broth
1¾	cups low-sodium canned beef broth
¼	cup dry red wine
2	sprigs fresh parsley
1	sprig fresh thyme
1	bay leaf
1	tablespoon balsamic vinegar
	Ground black pepper
1	baguette, cut on the bias into ¾-inch slices (2 slices per serving)
4½	ounces Swiss cheese, sliced ¹⁄₁₆ inch thick
3	ounces Asiago cheese, grated (about ¾ cup)

:: INSTRUCTIONS:

1. Melt butter in stockpot or Dutch oven over medium-high heat. Add onions and ½ teaspoon salt and stir to coat onions thoroughly with butter. Cook, stirring frequently, until onions are reduced and syrupy and inside of pot is coated with very deep brown crust, 30 to 35 minutes. Stir in chicken and beef broths, red wine, parsley, thyme, and bay leaf, scraping pot bottom with wooden spoon to loosen browned bits, and bring to a simmer. Simmer to blend flavors, about 20 minutes, and discard herbs. Stir in balsamic vinegar and adjust seasoning with salt and pepper to taste. (Soup can be refrigerated in airtight container up to 2 days; return to simmer before finishing with croutons and cheese).

2. To serve, adjust oven rack to upper-middle position and heat broiler. Set heatproof serving bowls or crocks on baking sheet and fill each with about 1½ cups soup. Top each bowl with two baguette slices and distribute Swiss cheese slices, placing them in a single layer, if possible, on bread. Sprinkle with about 2 tablespoons grated Asiago cheese and broil until well-browned and bubbly, about 10 minutes. Cool 5 minutes and serve.

chapter five

PUREED
VEGETABLE
SOUPS

INITIALLY, WE SET OUT TO DEVELOP A SINGLE master recipe for pureed vegetable soup, hoping that the same technique could be used with all vegetables. We quickly discovered that green vegetables, such as peas and asparagus, must be handled differently from the heartier, more starchy vegetables, such as carrots and butternut squash.

Dense winter vegetables are bulky enough to act as their own thickener. There is no need to add flour or cream to thicken soups made from these vegetables. Green vegetables, however, are not starchy enough to use on their own. They require flour and cream. Loss of color is another issue when making soups made from green vegetables. The two types of pureed soup are considered separately in this chapter.

SOUPS WITH HEARTY VEGETABLES

We enjoy the smooth, silky texture of creamed vegetable soups, but we often find the flavor to be lacking. The dairy elements (usually lots of butter and cream) mask the taste of the vegetables. Instead of an intense carrot flavor in a creamy base, for example, we usually taste cream with carrots in the background.

We wanted to see if there was a way to make a pureed soup that tasted more like vegetables. We wanted a creamy carrot soup reminiscent of the sweetest carrots, a butternut squash soup that really had the flavor of squash. And we were not willing to sacrifice anything in terms of consistency. Pureed vegetable soups must be silky. Otherwise, there is no point in pureeing them.

Most creamy vegetable soups contain flour. While we find flour to be essential when working with more watery green vegetables, starchy vegetables don't seem to need flour. In fact, when flour is added to soups made with dense, starchy vegetables, the texture becomes overly thick and starchy.

To find our way, we decided to use carrots as a model and then test other vegetables after developing a basic recipe. We started out by experimenting with other starches (cornstarch and potato starch) but found the results to be similar to soups made with flour. The texture was still too thick and gummy, and the vegetables were not the primary flavor. We had also seen recipes using potatoes or rice as thickeners, usually cooked right along with the vegetables in broth. When we tried this, though, the potatoes and rice detracted from the carrot flavor and caused the color of the soup to fade.

We found that the elimination of the starch improved the texture of the soup, but the recipe we were working with had a dairy component, and its flavor still dominated. It seemed to us that the best idea might be to use a larger quantity of vegetables and puree them for texture.

Most recipes for pureed vegetable soup use equal amounts of vegetables and liquid, or in some cases slightly more liquid than vegetables. We decided to alter this ratio in a big way and cook four cups of carrots in two cups of stock. We figured we would get more vegetable flavor and could use the vegetables themselves as a thickener.

This change resulted in an immediate improvement. By the time the vegetables were cooked, the mixture was thick enough to create a puree with good body. In fact, the pureed carrots and broth were actually a little too thick. Instead of adding cream to the vegetables as they cooked, we now needed to add cream to the blender to thin out the pureed carrots.

We used about one cup of cream to get the right consistency, but this was too much dairy fat for our taste. Next, we tried substituting half-and-half as well as whole and low-fat milk. We found that whole milk provided just the right amount of dairy fat to improve the texture, providing smoothness and a creamy mouthfeel without overwhelming the carrot flavor. Adding skim milk or 2 percent milk was like adding more broth—not at all satisfying. Half-and-half was good, but a tad too rich.

Now that we had successfully developed a bright orange carrot soup that tasted of good, sweet carrots, we wondered what other vegetables might take to this technique. Watery vegetables refused to work. Mushrooms, for instance, don't have enough fiber and bulk to work as their own thickening agent. Peas and asparagus are also poor candidates for this technique, which works best with tubers, roots, and hearty winter vegetables.

We have included recipes using carrots, butternut squash, and cauliflower, but the same technique can be applied to parsnips, turnips, beets, or sweet potatoes. These soups also taste delicious cold. To serve them cold, start off with oil instead of butter; unlike butter, the oil won't congeal when chilled.

Pureed Carrot Soup

serves four to six

➤ NOTE: *Use oil instead of butter when serving this soup cold.*

2	tablespoons unsalted butter or extra-virgin olive oil
1	medium onion, 3 medium shallots, or 1 medium leek (white and light green parts only), chopped
¼	cup dry sherry or white wine
1½	pounds (about 8 medium) carrots, peeled, halved lengthwise, and sliced thin (about 4 cups)
2	cups Chicken Stock (page 21) or low-sodium canned broth
1	teaspoon salt
⅛	teaspoon ground white pepper, or more to taste
	Pinch freshly grated nutmeg
1¼-1½	cups whole milk
2	teaspoons minced fresh tarragon, chives, or parsley leaves

∷ INSTRUCTIONS:

1. Heat butter or oil in large saucepan over medium heat. Add onion; sauté until golden, about 5 minutes. Stir in sherry and carrots; cook until sherry evaporates, about 30 seconds.

2. Add stock, salt, pepper, and nutmeg to saucepan; bring to a boil. Reduce heat to simmer, cover, and cook until carrots are tender, 20 to 25 minutes.

3. Ladle carrot mixture into blender. Add 1 cup milk; blend until very smooth. Return soup to saucepan; cook over low heat until warmed through. If soup is too thick, stir in up to ½ cup more milk to thin consistency. Adjust seasonings. Serve hot, garnishing bowls with minced herb.

VARIATIONS:

Pureed Butternut Squash Soup with Ginger

Follow recipe for Pureed Carrot Soup, adding 1 tablespoon finely minced fresh gingerroot to onions after onions have sautéed for 4 minutes. Continue cooking for 1 minute. Replace carrots with 1 medium butternut squash (about 2½ pounds), which has been halved, seeded, peeled, and cut into ½-inch cubes to yield 5 cups. Omit nutmeg and cook squash until tender, 15 to 20 minutes. Thin with 1 to 1¼ cups milk and garnish with minced chives or parsley.

Pureed Cauliflower Soup with Curry

Follow recipe for Pureed Carrot Soup, adding 1½ teaspoons curry powder to onions after onions have sautéed for 4 minutes. Continue cooking for 1 minute. Replace carrots with 1 medium head cauliflower (about 2 pounds), stems discarded and florets cut into bite-sized pieces to yield 5 cups. Omit nutmeg and cook cauliflower until tender, about 15 minutes. Thin with ¾ to 1 cup milk and garnish with minced chives or parsley.

SOUPS WITH GREEN VEGETABLES

Soups made with green vegetables behave quite differently from other pureed vegetable soups. Some green vegetables, such asparagus, are not starchy enough to create a thick texture when pureed. They need help from flour and/or cream. Loss of color is another key issue that affects all soups made with green vegetables.

Our goal was to develop pureed green vegetable soups with bright color and strong flavor. The color issue was fairly easy to solve. Green vegetables should not be simmered too long in soup. This means cutting the vegetables into small pieces so they cook quickly. Also, it is best to serve creamy green vegetable soups as soon as they are ready. Reheating is not kind to these soups, which are prone to turning a drab olive green.

The more problematic issue is flavor. As we found in earlier tests with carrots, flour and cream have a dulling effect on vegetable flavor. However, while carrots are sturdy enough to create a thick soup without either flour or cream, green vegetables are too watery. We tried to get around using flour and cream but were disappointed with the results. While soups made with starchy vegetables can become dull when thickened with these ingredients, pureed green vegetable soups are thin unless flour and cream are used. Our mission was clear: improve and enhance the veg-

5 0

etable flavor despite the need to add flour and cream.

We found that keeping simmering times to a minimum helped to preserve the flavor of green vegetables. Pureeing or finely chopping them in the food processor improved the texture of the soup and cut cooking time to a matter of minutes. For instance, we discovered that processing partly frozen peas in the food processor and simmering them briefly in the soup released their starch and flavor quickly. Boston lettuce, a common component in many pea soup recipes, gave our soup a marvelous, almost frothy texture.

For broccoli, the key was to pulse the trimmed stems and florets in the food processor. When cut so finely, broccoli will become completely tender in just seven or eight minutes of cooking, before its strong-smelling compounds have had a chance to form.

Asparagus proved more troublesome. No matter what we tried, the flavor in soups simmered for only a short time was too mild. When we allowed the asparagus to cook for a longer time (more than 15 minutes), the flavor was better, but the color was army green. We tried broiling the asparagus, hoping that this method would boost its flavor and help to break down its stringy texture. Broiled asparagus remained bright green and contributed much more flavor to the soup, but the texture was still too stringy.

We tried pureeing chopped raw asparagus before adding

it to the soup, and this greatly improved the texture. Unfortunately, the flavor of this soup paled in comparison with the soup made with broiled asparagus. The solution was simple: puree half of the asparagus for smooth texture and broil the other half for strong flavor. We found the results to be admirable; although the finished texture is not perfectly smooth—even after straining—the flavor and color are lovely.

Creamy Pea Soup

serves four to six

➤ **NOTE:** *Shallots work best with delicate green vegetables, but you can use an equal amount of onions or leeks.*

4	tablespoons unsalted butter
1	cup minced shallots (7 to 8 shallots)
2	tablespoons flour
4	cups Chicken Stock (page 21) or low-sodium canned broth
1½	pounds frozen peas, partially thawed at room temperature for 10 minutes
12	small Boston lettuce leaves (about 3 ounces), washed, dried, and chopped
½	cup heavy cream
	Salt and ground black pepper

INSTRUCTIONS:

1. Heat butter in large saucepan over medium-low heat. Add shallots and sauté, covered, until completely soft, 7 to 10 minutes, stirring occasionally. Stir in flour with wooden spoon. Cook for 30 seconds, stirring constantly. Add stock gradually, whisking constantly to thin out flour-butter mixture. Bring to a boil over medium-high heat, reduce heat to low, and simmer for 5 minutes.

53

2. While soup base is cooking, place partially frozen peas in workbowl of food processor and process until peas are texture of coarse, chopped pistachios, about 20 seconds. Stir peas and lettuce into soup base, cover, and bring to a simmer over medium-high heat. Uncover, reduce heat to medium, and simmer for 2 minutes.

3. Puree soup in a blender in two batches until smooth. Pour soup through fine strainer (see figure 1, page 15) and into clean saucepan, then stir in cream. Bring soup to a simmer, but do not boil. Season with salt and pepper to taste. Serve immediately.

▪▪ VARIATIONS:

Creamy Broccoli Soup

Follow step 1 of Creamy Pea Soup recipe, using 2 cups stock and 2 cups water. Trim tough bottom portion of stalks from 1 large bunch broccoli (about 1½ pounds). Peel tough outer skin from remaining portion of stalks. Coarsely chop peeled stalks and florets. Pulse broccoli in food processor until cut very small but not pureed. (The largest pieces should be pea-sized). Stir broccoli into soup base in place of peas and lettuce and simmer until tender, 7 to 8 minutes. Proceed with step 3 of Creamy Pea Soup recipe, but do not strain. Add 1½ teaspoons lemon juice with salt and pepper to taste.

Creamy Asparagus Soup

Preheat broiler and position rack on highest setting. Place 1½ pounds trimmed (tough ends discarded) asparagus on rimmed baking sheet. Drizzle 1 tablespoon melted butter over asparagus and roll asparagus back and forth to coat. Broil asparagus until tender and just beginning to color, about 5 minutes. Cool and roughly chop. Reserve. Chop another 1½ pounds raw, trimmed asparagus into 1-inch pieces and transfer to workbowl of food processor. Pulse until asparagus is finely chopped. Reserve separately.

Follow step 1 of Creamy Pea Soup recipe. Replace peas and lettuce in step 2 with broiled and raw chopped asparagus and simmer until tender, about 5 minutes. Proceed with step 3 of Creamy Pea Soup recipe. Add 1 tablespoon lemon juice with salt and pepper to taste. If soup seems too thick, add up to 1 cup hot water.

chapter six

CORN CHOWDER

THE BIGGEST CHALLENGE IN MAKING CORN chowder is getting corn flavor. The sweet, delicate flavor of corn can be easily overwhelmed by the cream, potatoes, leeks, bacon, and other seasonings. At the outset, we decided to use frozen corn because it is available year-round and is so easy to work with. (We also developed a variation for fresh corn that can be used during the summer.)

Since broiling worked so well to bring out the flavor of asparagus in our Creamy Asparagus Soup, we decided to try this method with frozen corn kernels. As we hoped, the flavor of the chowder made with broiled corn was richer and deeper. We had worried that the application of dry heat might toughen the kernels as well as enhance their flavor, but they softened nicely when stirred into the soup. As an added bonus, we found that broiled corn kernels were less likely to fall apart after being simmered.

Having achieved the corn flavor we were after, we turned our attention to texture. Many corn chowders are too thick, even gluey. We tried eliminating flour and the step of pureeing the finished soup, but did not like the results. The soup was a bit thin, and the corn and the liquid did not meld. Next, we tried pureeing the finished chowder, but we didn't like these results either. The soup was too dense, and we missed the chunks of corn and potato.

We decided to thicken the soup without pureeing. Sprinkling two tablespoons of flour over the sautéed aromatic vegetables worked well, but the soup was still a bit thin. When we added more flour, the soup tasted floury. We had better results when we pureed some of the corn kernels before adding them to the soup kettle. The starchy pureed corn made the soup silkier and heartier without making it dull or gluey. At last, we had a corn chowder with excellent corn flavor and a silky, substantial texture.

Corn Chowder

serves four to six

➤ **NOTE:** *Chowder made with frozen corn is delicious and easy to assemble. To use fresh corn, remove the kernels from five to six medium ears to yield the necessary five scant cups for this recipe.*

2	10-ounce packages frozen corn kernels (5 scant cups)
2	tablespoons vegetable oil
	Salt and ground black pepper
2	ounces (2 strips) bacon, cut crosswise into ¼-inch strips
3	tablespoons unsalted butter
2	medium leeks, white and light green parts, finely chopped
1	large celery stalk, cut into ¼-inch pieces
2	medium garlic cloves, minced
	Pinch cayenne pepper
2	tablespoons flour
4	cups Chicken Stock (page 21) or low-sodium canned broth
1	bay leaf
2	medium red potatoes, cut into ½-inch dice
1	teaspoon chopped fresh thyme leaves
1	cup heavy cream

:: INSTRUCTIONS:

1. Adjust oven rack to top position and heat broiler. Toss 4 scant cups corn with 1 tablespoon oil and salt and pepper to taste in large bowl. Spread corn out evenly over large baking sheet. Broil, stirring occasionally, until corn begins to brown, 7 to 10 minutes. Remove from oven and set aside. Allow remaining 1 scant cup corn to partially thaw, about 10 minutes. Process in food processor until very fine, about 15 seconds. Reserve.

2. Cook bacon in large saucepan or Dutch oven over medium heat until crisp, about 8 minutes. Remove bacon with slotted spoon and set aside. Pour off all bacon fat.

3. Melt butter in empty Dutch oven, still over medium heat. Add leeks and sauté until very soft, about 7 minutes. Add celery and cook for another 5 minutes, or until soft. Add garlic and cayenne; sauté until fragrant, about 1 minute. Stir in flour with wooden spoon. Cook for 2 minutes.

4. Add stock slowly, whisking constantly to thin flour-butter mixture. Add bay leaf and potatoes and bring to a boil. Reduce heat and simmer until potatoes are tender, 10 to 12 minutes. Add roasted corn, processed corn, and thyme; let soup simmer over medium-high heat for 5 minutes.

5. Stir in cream and return to a simmer. Add bacon and salt and pepper to taste. Remove bay leaf. Serve hot.

chapter seven

CREAM OF TOMATO SOUP

REAMY TOMATO SOUP SHOULD TASTE LIKE sweet, ripe tomatoes and have a rich red color. The cream should tame the acidity but not obliterate it. The soup should also be extremely smooth.

We knew that ripe August tomatoes would make excellent soup, but this recipe is really too heavy for summertime. It's best served at the holidays or for lunch on a cold winter's day, when only out-of-season tomatoes are available. We made five different tomato soup recipes using out-of-season fresh tomatoes, and the results were ghastly. All the soups were watery and tasted like cream and vegetables (onions, leeks, whatever was added to the base). The tomato flavor was so faint that the color was the only clue that the soups contained tomatoes.

Our next step was to test canned tomatoes. From past results, we knew that canned whole tomatoes packed in juice (not puree) have the freshest tomato flavor. That's because puree is a concentrate requiring higher and longer cooking times than simple canned tomatoes, whole or diced. We tried our favorite canned whole tomatoes (Muir Glen has been a consistent winner in our blind taste tests), and the results were better but not great. The soup needed more tomato flavor.

We wondered how we could get more flavor from canned tomatoes. We decided to trying broiling, which had worked well in soups made with corn and asparagus. The difference was enormous. The soup tasted as if it had been made with the finest, ripest summer tomatoes.

Admittedly, broiling canned tomatoes can be tricky. We had trouble with burning in some spots on the tray. We figured that roasting in a hot oven would deliver similar results without the risk of scorching. After several tests, we concluded that roasting at 450 degrees gave us excellent flavor without any scorching. Roasting both intensified the flavor of the canned tomatoes and mellowed their acidity.

With the all-important tomato element in place, we

wondered if we could intensify the flavor even further with tomato paste or sun-dried tomatoes. Sun-dried tomatoes added a bit more tomato flavor, but we felt the difference was not worth the bother of rehydrating the dried tomatoes in boiling water. The paste brought another level of tomato intensity to the soup and fortified the color. Paste is easy to add to the soup, so we have included some in our recipe.

Cream of Tomato Soup
serves four

➤ NOTE: *Roasting the canned tomatoes improves their flavor and gives the soup a rich red color.*

2	cans (28 ounces) whole tomatoes packed in juice, preferably Muir Glen
1½	tablespoons dark brown sugar
4	tablespoons unsalted butter
4	large shallots, minced (about ¾ cup)
1	tablespoon tomato paste
	Pinch ground allspice
2	tablespoons flour
2	cups Chicken Stock (page 21) or low-sodium canned broth, hot
½	cup heavy cream
2	tablespoons dry sherry or brandy
	Salt and cayenne pepper

▦ INSTRUCTIONS:

1. Adjust oven rack to middle position and heat oven to 450 degrees. Line a rimmed baking sheet with aluminum foil. Drain tomatoes in small strainer set over medium bowl. With your fingers, open whole tomatoes and remove seeds, allowing juices to fall through strainer and into bowl (see figure 6, right). Reserve 2 cups juice. Leaving seeds behind, transfer whole tomatoes to lined baking sheet and arrange in single layer (see figure 7, below right). Sprinkle tomatoes with brown sugar and bake until completely dry and starting to color, about 30 minutes. Let cool slightly, then peel tomatoes off foil. Reserve.

2. While tomatoes are roasting, melt butter in medium saucepan over medium heat until foaming. Add shallots, tomato paste, and allspice. Reduce heat to low, cover, and sauté, stirring occasionally, until shallots are completely soft, 7 to 10 minutes. Stir in flour and cook for 30 seconds, stirring constantly. Gradually add stock, whisking to incorporate the flour/butter mixture.

3. Add tomatoes and their juice. Cover and simmer gently for 10 minutes. Pour hot soup through strainer into clean saucepan. Puree solids left in strainer in blender with enough tomato broth in saucepan (about 1 cup) to achieve a perfectly smooth consistency. Stir puree into tomato broth and set pan over low heat. Add cream and sherry and season with salt and cayenne to taste. Bring to a simmer. Serve hot.

Figure 6.
With your fingers, carefully open the whole tomatoes over a
strainer set in a bowl and push out the seeds, allowing the juices
to fall through strainer and into the bowl. The seeded tomatoes
can go directly onto the baking sheet, as directed in figure 7.

Figure 7.
To promote even cooking, arrange the seeded tomatoes in a single layer
on a foil-lined, rimmed baking sheet. The foil is essential; it keeps the
tomatoes from scorching and sticking to the baking sheet.

65

chapter eight

POTATO-LEEK SOUP

OTATO-LEEK SOUP IS A STAPLE OF EUROPEAN peasant cooking. It is at once hearty and creamy because of the potatoes and lean because cream is rarely added. We had a number of questions. What kind of potatoes are best, and how should they should be cooked to keep them from disintegrating? How many leeks are necessary for good flavor? Should other alliums (onions and garlic) be added to the base?

We started by testing various kinds of potatoes. In our opinion, the potatoes in this soup should be tender but not mushy or waterlogged. In many of the recipes we tested, the potatoes fell apart into a starchy mess. Low-starch red potatoes are a must here. We discovered that they hold their shape better than russet potatoes or Yukon golds.

Precise timing for cooking the potatoes was hard to pinpoint. One minute the potatoes tasted a bit underdone, the next minute they were too soft. We hit upon the following solution: simmer the potatoes until the chunks are almost tender (there should be just a tiny bit of hardness in the center when tested), then turn off the heat, cover the pot, and let gentle residual heat finish cooking the potatoes.

With the potato issue settled, we moved on to the leeks. We started out with two leeks. Although this a common amount in many recipes, we found that soups with so few leeks tasted anemic. We concluded that while potatoes may add the texture and heft to this soup, the leeks are the real source of flavor. We eventually decided on five or six medium leeks, including some of the green section, which makes for a more robust flavor. We tried slicing the leeks quite fine as well as leaving the pieces fairly large. Larger pieces are a substantial and appealing addition to this soup.

We like the simplicity of using just leeks and potatoes but wondered if other vegetables (especially onions and garlic) might add flavor. We found the presence of garlic, even in small amounts or when roasted, to be overpowering. However, onions added another level of flavor that complemented that of the leeks.

Potato-Leek Soup
serves six to eight

➤ **NOTE:** *Red-skinned potatoes hold their shape better than other potatoes and are the best choice in this recipe.*

6	tablespoons unsalted butter
2	medium-large onions, chopped fine
5–6	medium leeks, whites and 3 inches of green section, halved lengthwise, washed, and cut crosswise into ¾-inch pieces (about 11 cups)
1	tablespoon flour
6	cups Chicken Stock (page 21) or low-sodium canned broth
1	bay leaf
1¾	pounds red potatoes, peeled and cut into ¾-inch dice (about 4 cups)
	Salt and ground black pepper

INSTRUCTIONS:

1. Melt butter in large Dutch oven over medium-low heat. When butter foams, add onions, cover, and cook, stirring occasionally, until very soft, about 10 minutes. Add leeks, increase heat to medium, cover, and cook, stirring occasionally, until tender but not mushy, 15 to 20 minutes. Do not allow leeks to color.

6 8

2. Sprinkle flour over vegetables and stir to coat evenly. Cook for 2 minutes. Gradually whisk in stock. Add bay leaf and potatoes, cover, and bring to a boil. Reduce heat and simmer, covered, until potatoes are almost tender, about 5 minutes. Remove pan from heat and keep covered until flavors meld and potatoes are completely tender, about 10 minutes. Remove bay leaf and season with salt and pepper to taste. Serve hot.

VARIATIONS:

Potato-Leek Soup with Kielbasa or Ham

Follow recipe for Potato-Leek Soup until potatoes are almost tender. Add 8 ounces kielbasa, cut into ¼-inch slices, or 8 ounces diced cooked ham, then cover pan and let flavors meld for 10 minutes. Proceed as directed.

Potato-Leek Soup with White Beans

Follow recipe for Potato-Leek Soup, reducing amount of potatoes to 1 pound. When potatoes are almost tender, add 1 cup cooked white beans and 1 cup hot water, cover pan, and let flavors meld for 10 minutes. Proceed as directed.

chapter nine

MINESTRONE

INESTRONE IS NOT A LIGHT UNDERTAK-ing. Any way you cut it, there is a lot of dicing and chopping. Given the amount of preparation, we thought it was important to discover which steps and ingredients were essential and which we could do without. Could everything be added to the pot at once, or is it necessary to precook some of the vegetables? Was stock essential, or could we use water, as do many traditional Italian recipes? How many vegetables were enough? And which ones?

While we wanted to pack the soup with vegetables, we were also determined to create a harmonious balance of flavors. Minestrone should be a team effort, with each element pulling equal weight. From the start, we decided to jettison vegetables that were too bold (such as broccoli) as well as those that were too bland and would contribute little flavor to the soup (such as button mushrooms).

We wanted to devise a basic technique for preparing the soup, and our research turned up two possible paths. The majority of recipes dump the vegetables into a pot with liquid and simmer them until everything is tender. A few recipes call for sautéing some or most of the vegetables before adding the liquid (along with any vegetables that would not benefit from cooking in fat, such as spinach).

Although we expected the soup with sautéed vegetables to be more flavorful, it wasn't. We then prepared three more pots without sautéing any of the vegetables. We added homemade vegetable stock to one pot, homemade chicken stock to a second, and water and the rind from a wedge of Parmesan cheese to the third.

The results were unexpected. The soup made with vegetable stock tasted one-dimensional and overwhelmingly sweet; because the vegetables were already sweet, using vegetable stock, which is also fairly sweet, did not help to balance the flavors. We realized we wanted the liquid portion of the soup to add a layer of complexity that would play off the vegetables. The soup made with chicken stock seemed to fit the bill. It was rich, complex, and delicious. However, the chicken flavor overwhelmed the vegetables. Diluting the stock with water wasn't the answer; this resulted in a rather bland soup. Ultimately, we preferred the soup made with water and the cheese rind. The Parmesan gave the broth a buttery, nutty flavor that contrasted nicely with the vegetables without overshadowing them.

We wanted the vegetables to soften completely but not lose their shape, and an hour of gentle simmering accomplished this. Much longer and the vegetables began to break down; any less time over the flame and the vegetables were too crunchy. We liked the concentrating effect of simmering without the lid on.

We also looked at several recipes that added some fresh vegetables at the end of the cooking time. This sounded like a nice idea, but the fresh peas and green beans added 10 minutes before the soup was done tasted uncooked and bland compared with the vegetables that had simmered in the flavorful soup for an hour. For maximum flavor, all the vegetables, even ones that usually require brief cooking times, should be added at the outset.

The addition of the cheese rind was an interesting find. During our research, we also turned up two other flavor boosters that could replace the cheese rind and be added to the soup from the start: rehydrated porcini mushrooms and their soaking liquid, and pancetta (unsmoked Italian bacon). The pancetta proved to be a better team player.

Pancetta must be sautéed to render its fat and release its flavor. We cooked a little pancetta until crisp in some olive oil, then added the water and vegetables. Like the cheese rind, the pancetta contributed depth. But while cheese rind gave the soup a buttery, nutty flavor, the pancetta added a very subtle flavor of pork and spice. We tried regular American bacon as well. It was a bit stronger and lent a smoky element to the soup. In the recipe variation below, we prefer the subtler flavor of the pancetta, but either pancetta or smoked bacon make for a much more flavorful soup than one made with water alone.

Up until this point, we had focused on ingredients that went into the soup pot at the start. But many traditional Mediterranean recipes stir in fresh herbs or herb pastes just before the soup is served. Pesto is the most common choice, and we were hooked from the first time we added it to the soup. The heat of the soup releases the perfume of the basil and garlic and creates another delicious layer of flavor. A simple mixture of minced fresh rosemary, garlic, and extra-virgin olive oil was also delicious. As with the pesto, the oil adds some fat to a soup that is otherwise very lean. The rosemary and garlic combo is very strong and must be used in smaller quantities than the pesto.

Minestrone
serves six to eight

➤ **NOTE:** *The rind from a wedge of Parmesan cheese, prefer-ably Parmigiano-Reggiano, brings complexity and depth to a soup made with water instead of stock. Remove the rind from a wedge of fresh Parmesan, or save the rinds from pieces that have been completely grated in a zipper-lock bag, stored in the freezer to use as needed.*

2	small leeks (or 1 large), washed thoroughly, white and light green parts sliced thin, crosswise
2	medium carrots, chopped small
2	small onions, chopped small
2	medium celery stalks, chopped small
1	medium baking potato, peeled and cut into medium dice
1	medium zucchini, cut into medium dice
3	cups stemmed spinach leaves, cut into thin strips
1	can (28 ounces) whole tomatoes packed in juice, drained, and chopped
1	Parmesan cheese rind, about 5 x 2 inches
	Salt
1	can (15 ounces) cannellini beans, drained and rinsed
¼	cup pesto or 1 tablespoon minced fresh rosemary mixed with 1 teaspoon minced garlic and 1 tablespoon extra-virgin olive oil
	Ground black pepper

▓▓ INSTRUCTIONS:

1. Bring vegetables, tomatoes, 8 cups water, cheese rind, and 1 teaspoon salt to boil in a stockpot. Reduce heat to medium-low; simmer uncovered, stirring occasionally until vegetables are tender but still hold their shape, about 1 hour. (At this point, soup can be refrigerated in airtight container for 3 days or frozen for 1 month.)

2. Add beans and cook just until heated through, about 5 minutes. Remove pot from heat. Remove and discard cheese rind. Stir in pesto or rosemary-garlic mixture. Adjust seasonings, adding pepper and more salt, if necessary. Serve immediately.

▓▓ VARIATIONS:

Minestrone with Pancetta

Mince 2 ounces thinly sliced pancetta or bacon and sauté in 1 tablespoon extra-virgin olive oil in soup kettle until crisp, 3 to 4 minutes. Proceed with recipe for Minestrone, adding vegetables, tomatoes, and water but omitting cheese rind.

Minestrone with Rice or Pasta

Follow recipe for Minestrone or Minestrone with Pancetta until vegetables are tender. Add ½ cup Arborio rice or small pasta shape, such as elbows or orzo, and continue cooking until rice is tender, about 20 minutes, or until pasta is al dente, 8 to 12 minutes. Add beans and proceed as directed.

VARYING MINESTRONE

Minestrone contains seven kinds of vegetables as well as tomatoes and cannellini beans. The aromatics—leeks, carrots, onions, and celery—are essential, as are the tomatoes. We like to add starchy potatoes, sweet zucchini, and leafy spinach, but these choices can be altered according to personal preference.

What follows are some notes on other vegetables that were tested in this soup. Bell peppers and broccoli were too distinctive, while eggplant and white mushrooms added little flavor, so none of these four vegetables is recommended.

When making substitutions, keep in mind that the Minestrone recipe has 2½ cups of solid vegetables (potatoes and zucchini) and three cups of leafy spinach. Use similar proportions when working with the vegetables below.

As for the beans, white kidney beans, called cannellini beans in Italy, are the classic choice. But other white beans can be used, as well as red kidney, cranberry, or borlotti beans, all of which appear in various Italian recipes for minestrone.

CAULIFLOWER: While broccoli is too intense for minestrone, milder cauliflower can blend in. Cut into tiny florets and use in place of potatoes or zucchini.

ESCAROLE: This slightly bitter green works well with white beans and pasta. Chop and use in place of spinach.

GREEN BEANS: Beans are a standard ingredient in French versions of this soup. Cut into ½-inch pieces and use in place of zucchini.

KALE: This assertive green can be overwhelming on its own, but it gives the soup a pleasant edge when combined with spinach. Remove ribs and chop. Use up to 1½ cups in place of 1½ cups of spinach.

PEAS: The delicate flavor of fresh peas is wasted in this soup, so use frozen. Add up to ½ cup in place of ½ cup zucchini or white beans.

SAVOY CABBAGE: This crinkly leaf cabbage adds an earthy note. Shred finely and use up to 1½ cups in place of 1½ cups spinach.

SWISS CHARD: This green is similar to spinach, with a slightly more earthy flavor. Remove ribs and chop. Use in place of spinach.

TURNIPS: The modest bitter edge of the turnip helps balance out the flavors of the sweet vegetables. Peel and use in place of potatoes.

WINTER SQUASH: Butternut squash is sweet, but in small quantities it is especially colorful and delicious. Peel and dice. Use in place of potatoes or zucchini.

chapter ten

LENTIL SOUP

OUR IDEAL LENTIL SOUP IS THICK AND hearty, with lentils that are still intact. Many of the recipes we tested made delicious soups, but their texture was unappealing because the lentils had disintegrated into a thick mush.

We started our testing by focusing on the type of lentil. Red lentils fall apart when simmered and are best used in purees. We had better luck with the common brown lentils (sometimes tinged with green) that are sold in supermarkets. Although not perfect, our initial tests revealed that they make a better soup than red lentils. We had the best results with French green lentils, called lentils du Puy. They stay particularly firm when cooked, making them ideal for soups.

Since most supermarkets don't carry French green lentils, we decided to see if we could devise a method for handling common brown lentils that would make them less likely to fall apart when cooked. Our first area of research was salt.

Many sources recommend adding salt only after the lentils have been cooked, warning that they will toughen otherwise. We wondered if adding salt at the outset might make them less likely to disintegrate. We added salt at the outset, at the halfway point, and at the end of the cooking time and found no difference in texture. However, lentils cooked in liquid that was salted at the outset tasted better, having a more developed flavor.

Several sources suggested sautéing the lentils in oil before adding liquid to strengthen the outer skins. This technique works with rice—it is used to make pilaf and risotto—and it seemed worth a try. We found that lentils cooked for a while without liquid did in fact hold up better to the simmering process. When the soup was done, sautéed lentils were firmer than lentils added directly to the liquid without prior cooking. It seems that sautéing does indeed harden the lentil's outside layer of starch, producing a soup with tender lentils that do not fall apart.

Lentil Soup

serves four to six

➤ **N O T E :** *Common brown lentils work well in this recipe, although French green lentils are even better.*

2	tablespoons vegetable oil
4	slices (about 4 ounces) bacon, diced
2	medium-large onions, chopped fine
2	medium carrots, peeled and chopped medium
3	medium garlic cloves, minced
1	bay leaf
1	teaspoon minced fresh thyme leaves
1	can (14.5 ounces) diced tomatoes, drained and liquid reserved
1	cup lentils, rinsed and picked through to remove any stones
1	teaspoon salt
	Ground black pepper
¾	cup white wine
4	cups Chicken Stock (page 21) or low-sodium canned broth
1	tablespoon balsamic vinegar (optional)

▒ I N S T R U C T I O N S :

1. Heat oil in large, heavy-bottomed saucepan over medium-high heat. When oil is shimmering, add bacon and stir, cooking until fat is fully rendered and bacon is crisp, 3 to 4 minutes. Add onions, carrots, garlic, bay leaf, thyme, and drained tomatoes, and cook until vegetables begin to soften, about 2 minutes.

2. Stir in lentils, salt, and pepper to taste. Cover, reduce heat to medium-low, and sweat vegetables until softened, 8 to 10 minutes; lentils will become darker in color.

3. Uncover, increase heat to high, add wine, and simmer for 1 minute. Add stock, juice from canned tomatoes, and 1½ cups water. Bring to a boil, partially cover, and reduce heat to low, simmering until lentils are cooked but still hold their shape, 30 to 35 minutes. Remove and discard bay leaf.

4. Place 3 cups soup in blender and puree until smooth. Add pureed soup back to saucepan, and stir in vinegar, if using. Serve hot.

chapter eleven

HAM AND SPLIT PEA SOUP

W E LOVE SPLIT PEA SOUP MADE WITH ham broth; the problem is that nowadays, except for the occasional holiday, most cooks rarely buy a bone-in ham. We wondered if we could duplicate this wonderful soup without buying a huge ham.

To confirm or disprove our belief that ham broth is crucial to split pea soup, we made several pork broths and pork-enhanced canned chicken broths. In addition to making broth the old-fashioned way, from a meaty ham bone, we made broths from smoked pork necks, pork hocks (fresh and smoked), and smoked ham shanks. We also made cheater broths: kielbasa simmered in canned chicken broth, kielbasa simmered in water, bacon simmered in chicken broth, and bacon simmered in water.

Broths made with hocks—fresh as well as smoked— were more greasy than flavorful. In addition, the hocks gave up very little meat, making it necessary to purchase an additional portion of ham to fortify the soup. Ham shanks, which include the hock, made a pleasant but lightweight broth that was a tad greasy and salty—both fixable problems had we liked the broth more. Pork necks, which are not widely available, made a fairly flavorful but salty broth. All four cheater broths failed. Both the kielbasa- and bacon-enhanced chicken broths tasted strongly of overly processed meat, while the water-based versions tasted weak.

Not surprisingly, the broth made from the bone of a big ham was the winner. It was meaty and full-flavored, rich but not greasy, nicely seasoned without being overly salty, and smoky without tasting artificial. Unlike any of the other broths, this one sported bits of meat. And not just good meat—great meat. The tender pieces of ham that fell away from the bone during cooking were not just a nice byproduct of the broth. They were the glory of our split pea soup. But was there a way around buying half a ham (with an average weight of about 8 pounds) just to make a pot of soup?

After checking out the ham and smoked pork cases at

83

several different stores, we discovered the picnic ham from the pork shoulder. Unlike the cut we generally refer to as ham, which comes from the back legs of the animal, the picnic comes from the shoulder and front legs. Smaller than a ham, the half-picnic weighs only 4½ pounds. After making a couple more pots of soup, we found that the picnic pork shoulder—with its bones, fat, rind, and meat—made outstanding stock, and after two hours of simmering, the meat was meltingly tender yet still potently flavorful.

Since we did not need the full picnic half for our pot of soup, we pulled off and roasted two of its meatier muscles and used the remaining meat, bone, fat, and rind to make the soup. At around 99 cents a pound, a picnic shoulder is usually cheaper than a ham, and often cheaper than pork hocks, shanks, and neck bones as well. Here, we thought, was the modern solution. Rather than buy a ham for eating (and eating and eating) with a leftover bone for soup, buy a picnic for making soup, then roast the remaining couple of pounds for eating.

There are several ways to make ham and split pea soup. You can throw all the ingredients—ham bone, peas, and diced vegetables—into a pot and simmer until everything is tender. Or you can sauté the vegetables, then add the remaining ingredients, and cook the soup until the ham and peas are tender. Alternatively, you can cook the ham bone and peas (or give the ham bone a little bit of a head start) until ham and peas are tender and then add raw, sautéed, or caramelized vegetables to the pot, continuing to cook until the vegetables are tender and the flavors have blended.

Although we had hoped to make this soup a straight forward one-pot operation, we found that dumping everything in at the same time resulted in gloppy, overcooked peas and tired mushy vegetables by the time the ham was tender. For textural contrast in this smooth, creamy soup, we ultimately preferred fully—not overly—cooked vegetables.

Our best soups were those in which the vegetables spent enough time in the pot for their flavors to blend but not so long that they had lost all of their individuality. Of the soups with vegetables added toward the end of cooking, we preferred the one with the caramelized vegetables. The sweeter vegetables gave this otherwise straightforward meat and starch soup a richness and depth of flavor that made the extra step and pan worth the trouble.

Many pea soup recipes call for an acidic ingredient—vinegar, lemon juice, fortified wines such as sherry or Madeira, Worcestershire sauce, or sour cream—to bring balance to an otherwise rich, heavy soup. After tasting all of the above, we found ourselves drawn to balsamic vinegar. Unlike any of the other ingredients, balsamic vinegar's mildly sweet, mildly acidic flavor perfectly complemented the soup.

Ham and Split Pea Soup

serves six

➤ NOTE: *Use a small 2½–pound smoked picnic portion ham if you can find one. Otherwise, buy a half-picnic ham and remove some meat (see figures 8 and 9, page 89), which you can save for use in sandwiches, salads, or omelets.*

1	piece (about 2½ pounds) smoked, bone-in picnic ham
4	bay leaves
1	pound (2½ cups) split peas, rinsed and picked through to remove any stones
1	teaspoon dried thyme
2	tablespoons extra-virgin olive oil
2	medium onions, chopped medium
2	medium carrots, chopped medium
2	medium celery stalks, chopped medium
1	tablespoon butter
2	medium garlic cloves, minced
	Pinch sugar
3	small new potatoes, scrubbed and cut into medium dice
	Ground black pepper
	Minced red onion (optional)
	Balsamic vinegar

86

INSTRUCTIONS:

1. Bring 3 quarts water, ham, and bay leaves to boil, covered, over medium-high heat in large soup kettle. Reduce heat to low and simmer until meat is tender and pulls away from bone, 2 to 2½ hours. Remove ham meat and bone from broth; add split peas and thyme and simmer until peas are tender but not dissolved, about 45 minutes. Meanwhile, when ham is cool enough to handle, shred meat into bite-sized pieces and set aside. Discard rind and bone.

2. While ham is simmering, heat oil in large skillet over high heat until shimmering. Add onions, carrots, and celery; sauté, stirring frequently, until most of the liquid evaporates and vegetables begin to brown, 5 to 6 minutes. Reduce heat to medium-low; add butter, garlic, and sugar. Cook vegetables, stirring frequently, until deeply browned, 30 to 35 minutes; set aside.

3. Add sautéed vegetables, potatoes, and shredded ham to soup; simmer until potatoes are tender and peas dissolve and thicken soup to the consistency of light cream, about 20 minutes more. Remove and discard bay leaves. Season with pepper to taste. Serve hot, sprinkling red onion over bowls, if desired, and passing vinegar separately at table.

VARIATION:

Ham and Split Pea Soup with Caraway

Toast 1½ teaspoons caraway seeds in a small skillet over medium-high heat, stirring frequently, until fragrant and browned, about 4 minutes. Follow recipe for Ham and Split Pea Soup, substituting toasted caraway seeds for the dried thyme.

Figure 8.

A half-picnic ham is readily available in supermarkets but contains too much meat for a pot of soup. Our solution is to pull off several meaty sections of the ham and save the meat for sandwiches, salads, or egg dishes. With your fingers, loosen the large comma-shaped muscles on top of the picnic half.

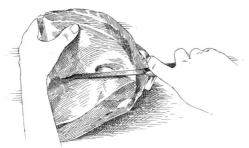

Figure 9.

Use a knife to cut the membrane separating the comma-shaped muscles from the rest of the roast. The remaining meat and bone can be used to make soup.

chapter twelve

NEW ENGLAND
CLAM CHOWDER

W E WANTED TO DEVELOP A DELICIOUS, traditional chowder that was economical, would not curdle, and could be prepared quickly. Before testing recipes, we explored our clam options. Because chowders are typically made with hard-shell clams, we purchased a variety (from smallest to largest): cockles, littlenecks, cherrystones, and chowder clams, often called quahogs.

Although littlenecks and cockles made delicious chowders, we eliminated them; both were just too expensive to toss into a chowder pot. Chowders made with the cheapest clams, however, weren't really satisfactory, either. The quahogs we purchased for testing were large (four to five inches in diameter), tough, and strong-flavored. Their oversized bellies (and the contents therein) gave the chowder an overbearing mineral taste that frustrated our efforts to develop a smooth, rich flavor.

Though only a little more expensive, cherrystones offer good value and flavor. The chowder made from these slightly smaller clams was distinctly clam-flavored, without an inky aftertaste. Because there are no industry sizing standards for each clam variety, you may find some small quahogs labeled as cherrystones or large cherrystones labeled as quahogs. No matter what their designation, clams much over three inches in diameter will deliver a distinctly metallic chowder.

Steaming clams open is far easier than shucking them. Five minutes over simmering water, and the clams open as naturally as a budding flower. Ours did not toughen up as long as we pulled them from the pot as soon as they opened and didn't let them cook too long in the finished chowder.

The extra step of purging, or filtering, hard-shell clams is unnecessary. All of the hard-shells we tested were relatively clean, and what little sediment there was sank to the bottom of the steaming liquid. Getting rid of the grit was as simple as leaving the last few tablespoons of broth in the pan when pouring it from the pot. If you find that your clam broth is gritty, strain it through a coffee filter.

Older recipes call for thickening clam chowder with crumbled biscuits; bread crumbs and crackers are modern stand-ins. Standard chowders thickened with bread crumbs or crackers failed to impress. We wanted a smooth, creamy soup base for the potatoes, onions, and clams, but no matter how long the chowder was simmered, neither the bread crumbs nor the crackers ever completely dissolved into the cooking liquid. Heavy cream alone, by contrast, did not give the chowder enough body. We discovered fairly quickly that flour would be necessary, not only as a thickener but as a stabilizer; unthickened chowders separate and curdle.

Because chowders call for potatoes, some cooks suggest that starchy baking potatoes, which tend to break down when boiled, can double as a thickener. We found that the potatoes did not break down sufficiently but instead simply became mushy. Red boiling potatoes are best for chowders.

Should the chowder be enriched with milk or cream? We found that so much milk was required to make it look and taste creamy that the chowder started to lose its clam flavor, becoming more like mild bisque or the clam equivalent of oyster stew. Making the chowder with almost all clam broth (five cups of the cooking liquid from the steaming clams) and then finishing it with a cup of cream gave us what we were looking for—a rich, creamy chowder that tasted distinctly of clams.

New England Clam Chowder

serves six

➤ **NOTE**: *You can replace the bacon with 4 ounces of salt pork.*

7	pounds medium-sized hard-shell clams, such as cherrystones, washed and scrubbed clean
4	slices thick-cut bacon (about 4 ounces), cut into ¼-inch pieces
1	large Spanish onion, diced medium
2	tablespoons flour
3	medium red potatoes (about 1½ pounds), scrubbed and diced medium
1	large bay leaf
1	teaspoon fresh thyme leaves or ¼ teaspoon dried thyme
1	cup heavy cream
2	tablespoons minced fresh parsley leaves
	Salt and ground black or white pepper

INSTRUCTIONS:

1. Bring clams and 3 cups water to boil in large, covered stock-pot. Steam until clams just start to open (see figure 10, page 95), 3 to 5 minutes. Transfer clams to large bowl; cool slightly. Open clams with a paring knife, holding clams over bowl to catch any juices. With knife, sever muscle that attaches clam to shell (see figure 11, page 95); transfer meat to cutting board.

9 3

Mince clams; set aside. Pour clam broth into 2-quart Pyrex measuring cup, holding back last few tablespoons broth in case of sediment; set clam broth aside. (You should have about 5 cups.) Rinse and dry pot; return to burner.

2. Fry bacon in pot over medium-low heat until fat renders and bacon crisps, 5 to 7 minutes. Add onion to bacon; sauté until softened, about 5 minutes. Add flour; stir until lightly colored, about 1 minute. Gradually whisk in reserved clam juice. Add potatoes, bay leaf, and thyme; simmer until potatoes are tender, about 10 minutes. Add clams, cream, parsley, and salt (if necessary) and pepper to taste; bring to simmer. Remove from heat and serve immediately.

∷ VARIATION:

Quick Pantry Clam Chowder

If you're short on time or find clams to be scarce and expensive, we've found that the right canned clams and bottled clam juice can deliver a chowder that's at least three notches above canned soup in quality. We tested seven brands of minced and small whole canned clams. We preferred Doxsee Minced Clams teamed with Doxsee brand clam juice. Doxsee clams were neither too tough nor too tender, and they had a decent, natural, clam flavor.

Follow recipe for New England Clam Chowder, substituting for fresh clams 4 cans (6.5 ounces each) minced

9 4

clams, juice drained and reserved, plus 1 cup water and 2 bottles (8 ounces each) clam juice. Add clam juice and meat at points when fresh clam juice and meat would be added.

Figure 10.
Steam clams until just open, at left, rather than completely open, as shown at right.

Figure 11.
Carefully use a paring knife to open clams, holding each over a bowl to catch the juices. When open, discard the top shell and use the knife to sever the muscle that connects the clams to the bottom shell.

95

index